PRIMARY SOURCES OF
FAMOUS PEOPLE IN AMERICAN HISTORY™

JOHN SUTTER

CALIFORNIA PIONEER

CHRIS HAYHURST

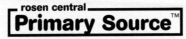

rosen central
Primary Source™

The Rosen Publishing Group, Inc., New York

Published in 2004 by The Rosen Publishing Group, Inc.
29 East 21st Street, New York, NY 10010

First Edition

Library of Congress Cataloging-in-Publication Data
Hayhurst, Chris.
John Sutter / Christopher Hayhurst.— 1st ed.
   p. cm. — (Primary Sources of Famous people in American history)
Summary: Surveys the life of Swiss/German immigrant John Sutter, on whose land gold was discovered in the mid-nineteenth century, spurring the California gold rush and westward expansion.
Includes bibliographical references (p.) and index.
ISBN 0-8239-4114-0 (lib. bdg.)
ISBN 0-8239-4186-8 (pbk. bdg.)
6-pack ISBN 0-8239-4313-5
1. Sutter, John Augustus, 1803-1880—Juvenile literature. 2. Pioneers—California—Biography—Juvenile literature. 3. Swiss Americans—California—Biography—Juvenile literature. 4. California—Gold discoveries—Juvenile literature. 5. California—History—1846-1850—Juvenile literature. 6. Sutter's Fort (Sacramento, Calif.)—Juvenile literature. [1. Sutter, John Augustus, 1803-1880. 2. Pioneers. 3. California—History—To 1846. 4.California—History—1846-1850.] I. Title. II. Series.
F865.S93H395 2003
979.4'04'092—dc21

                                                                                    2003002133

Manufactured in the United States of America

Photo credits: cover © California Department of Parks and Recreation; p. 4 courtesy of Map Division, The New York Public Library, Astor, Lenox, and Tilden Foundations; p. 5 © Hulton-Deutsch Collection/Corbis; p. 6 © Christel Gerstenberg/Corbis; pp. 7, 25, 27 Culver Pictures; pp. 8, 21, 23 © Hulton/Archive/Getty Images; p. 9 © Gianni Dagli Orti/Corbis; p. 11 The Phelps Stokes Collection, Miriam and Ira D. Wallach Division of Art, Prints and Photographs, The New York Public Library, Astor, Lenox, and Tilden Foundations; p. 12 Chris Logan; p. 13 courtesy of the Rare Books and Manuscripts Collection, The New York Public Library, Astor, Lenox, and Tilden Foundations; p. 15 Library of Congress Geography and Map Division; p. 17 Library of Congress, Prints & Photographs Division, HABS, CAL,34-SAC,57-17; p. 19 Library of Congress, Prints & Photographs Division; pp. 20, 24 © Bettmann/Corbis; p. 28 © Maura B. McConnell; p. 29 © Lowell Georgia/Corbis.

Designer: Thomas Forget; Photo Researchers: Rebecca Anguin-Cohen and Peter Tomlinson

CONTENTS

1 THE WORLD WELCOMES AN ADVENTURER

John Sutter was born on February 15, 1803, in a German town called Baden. Most of John's family was from Switzerland.

In 1818, John's parents sent him to Switzerland to go to school. When he was finished, he moved to the Swiss city of Basel. One day he met a woman named Anna Dübeld and fell in love.

A map of Europe showing Germany and Switzerland. Like Sutter, many Europeans immigrated to America in search of a better life.

A view of Basel, Switzerland, on the Rhine River. After the Napoleonic Wars, Switzerland seemed peaceful and prosperous.

John and Anna were married in 1826. They immediately began raising a family. To make money, John worked as a printer. Unfortunately, he did not do well. Soon John owed people lots of money.

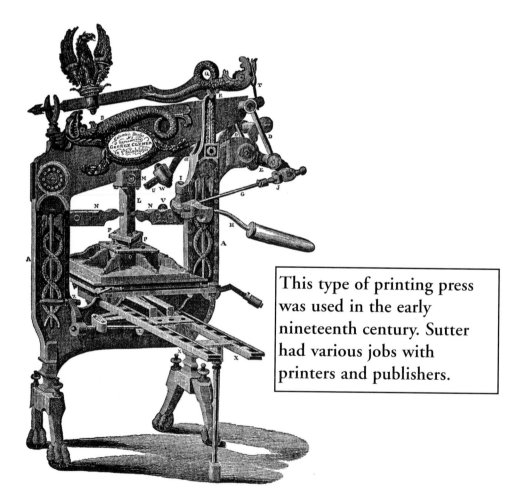

This type of printing press was used in the early nineteenth century. Sutter had various jobs with printers and publishers.

John Sutter in his Swiss army uniform before immigrating to the United States.

In 1828, Sutter volunteered for the Swiss army. By 1834, Sutter owed so much he feared he would be arrested. To escape the police, he left Anna and the children and sailed for the United States. He hoped he would find wealth in the New World.

A newspaper illustration depicts an immigrant ship crossing the Atlantic. Immigrants are crowded into the forward main deck.

EMIGRANT NEEDLEWOMEN ON DECK.

Soldiers in the Swiss army in the early nineteenth century.
Sutter joined the Swiss army to escape his creditors. Soon
emigration seemed more attractive than army life.

2 AMERICA

Sutter's ship docked in New York in July 1834. He began traveling west. Sutter told people he was an officer in the Swiss army. "Call me Captain John Sutter," he said, even though he was not a captain. His first stop was in Missouri. He was low on cash, so he sold some of his possessions. He took the money he made to buy goods he could trade.

WHEN LAND MEANT FREEDOM

Most immigrants did not come to America to live in the cities, but to go west, obtain their own land, and farm for a living. Sutter received a huge grant of land (50,000 acres) from the Mexican government for his settlement.

These are ships in New York Harbor, as seen from the area around Brooklyn Heights. In the age of sail, an immigrant's journey was long and dangerous.

"Captain Sutter" was a natural at the trading business. He traveled from Missouri to the Mexican town of Santa Fe. There he traded goods for valuables like mules. Back in Missouri, the animals were worth lots of money.

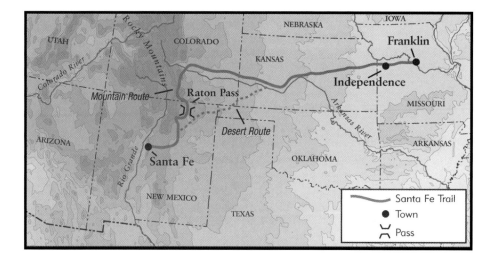

This is a map of the Santa Fe Trail, one of several major routes west for settlers, immigrants, and merchants.

Missouri traders rolled along the Santa Fe Trail in Conestoga wagons. John Sutter was such a trader for a number of years.

Sutter's wealth grew. But some people accused him of cheating and stealing. Sutter promised he would pay everyone back. But he never did. One day in 1838, he decided to leave town for good. He packed his bags and headed for California. California was then part of Mexico. Sutter would start a colony of settlers and become rich.

DID YOU KNOW?

In the 1800s, settlers were required to live in Mexico for one year before they could become Mexican citizens. On August 29, 1840, almost exactly a year after his arrival in California, Sutter received his papers and became a Mexican citizen.

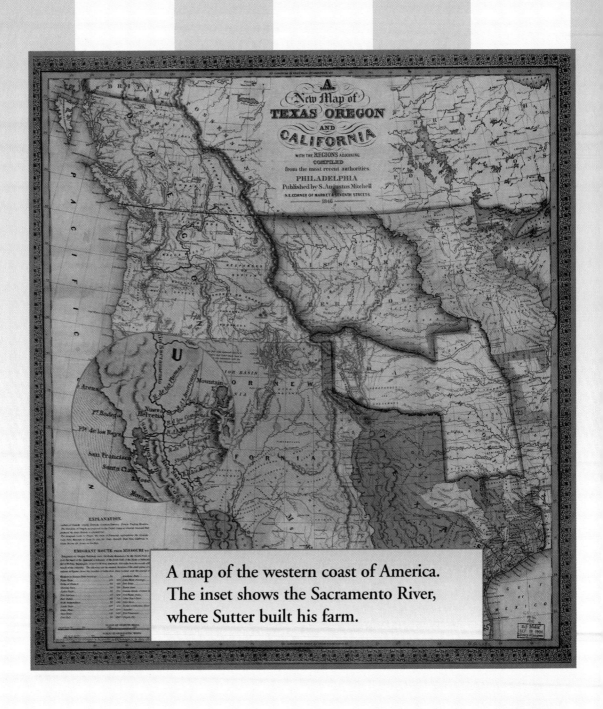

A map of the western coast of America. The inset shows the Sacramento River, where Sutter built his farm.

3 A DREAM COMES TRUE

In 1839, Sutter's journey west led him to Monterey. Monterey was the capital of California. Monterey's governor gave him permission to build his settlement. He showed Sutter a map. He pointed to a spot along the Sacramento River. There were Native Americans there, but there were also nearly 50,000 acres of land.

MOVING WESTWARD

When Sutter came west on the Santa Fe Trail in the 1830s, many Native American tribes were hostile to the settlers, and it was a dangerous journey. Fighting between Native Americans and settlers continued until well after the Civil War.

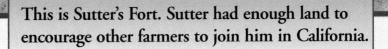

This is Sutter's Fort. Sutter had enough land to encourage other farmers to join him in California.

Sutter named the area New Helvetia. Using Native Americans and other laborers, he built Sutter's Fort. Soon his colony had farms and thousands of cattle, horses, and sheep.

Sutter called for more settlers to join the colony. He promised those who would stay that they could have work and free land.

WHAT'S IN A NAME?

Sutter's New Helvetia was named in honor of his European roots. The name means "New Switzerland."

This is another view of Sutter's Fort, New Helvetia, from a lithograph by William E. Endicott, 1849.

In 1846, war broke out between the United States and Mexico. Near the war's end, the United States took control of California. It would be easier for Americans to move west. Sutter invited settlers to come to New Helvetia. But then something happened that would change his life forever.

Mexican General Antonio Lopez de Santa Anna led Mexican forces against the American invasion of his country in 1846.

American troops storm the Heights of Monterrey in 1846, during the Mexican-American War. Americans won the war and annexed New Mexico and California.

4 GOLD!

One day a carpenter who worked for Sutter looked down and saw what looked like gold. He took the gold to Sutter. Sutter told the worker to keep the discovery a secret. The secret got out. Soon word of the gold spread to San Francisco. The Gold Rush was on. People from all over rushed to California.

THE GARDEN OF CALIFORNIA

The land Sutter abandoned in California would become one of the most productive fruit and vegetable growing regions in the country. If he had stayed, he might have become rich.

In this scene, men are panning for gold in California. Heavy gold particles would collect on the bottom of a pan when the dirt and other materials were washed away.

New Helvetia was overrun by thousands of people. Sutter's workers left him to look for gold. His colony was nearly destroyed in the frenzy. In 1849, Sutter abandoned his fort and moved to a farm.

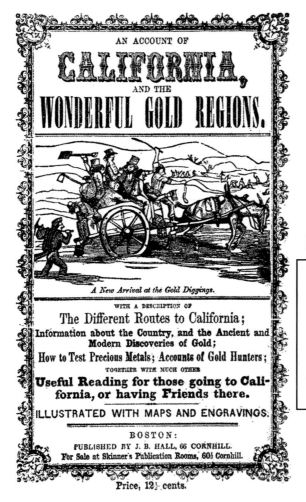

This is the title page from an 1849 manual on gold mining. Gold encouraged many people to come west and settle in California.

A picture of the farm Sutter moved to after he abandoned New Helvetia. He did not profit from the Gold Rush.

Finally, in 1850, Sutter's family came to the United States. They thought he would be living in luxury. Instead, he was a failed businessman. Captain Sutter was financially ruined.

THE NEW GENERATION

John and Anna Sutter had four children. Their names were Johann Augustus Jr., Anna Eliza, Emil Viktor, and Wilhelm Alphonse.

This photo of John Sutter was taken late in his life, after bankruptcy and retirement. Sutter had a difficult life, having settled in the wrong place at the wrong time.

Sutter spent the rest of his life trying to repay his debts. In 1865, the Sutters' house burned down. John and Anna decided to leave California. They moved to Washington, D.C., and then to Lititz, Pennsylvania. On June 18, 1880, John died. Anna died six months later. Today their graves can be found in a small cemetery in Lititz.

GENL. JOHN A. SUTTER.
BORN FEB. 28TH 1803.
AT KANDERN BADEN.
DIED JUNE 18TH 1880.
AT WASHINGTON. D.C.
REQUIESCAT IN PACEM

ANNA SUTTER NÉE DÜBELD.
BORN SEPT. 15TH 1805.
SWITZERLAND.
DIED JAN. 19TH 1881.
AT LITITZ.

The grave site of John Sutter and his wife in Lititz, Pennsylvania. When they arrived in America, his wife and children found him penniless.

A modern reconstruction of Sutter's Fort near Sacramento. The Gold Rush made California one of the most populous states.

TIMELINE

1803—John Sutter is born.

1818—Sutter starts school in Switzerland.

1826—Sutter marries Anna Dübeld.

1828—Sutter volunteers for service in the Swiss army.

1834—Sutter arrives in the United States and travels west.

1839—Sutter arrives in Monterey, California, and starts his settlement.

1846—The Mexican-American War begins.

1849—Sutter leaves New Helvetia.

1865—The Sutters move to Washington, D.C.

1880—Sutter dies at the age of 76.

GLOSSARY

colony (KAH-luh-nee) A group of people living in a new place.
Europe (YOOR-uhp) One of the seven continents.
financial (fy-NAN-shuhl) Having to do with money.
frenzy (FREHN-zee) Wild activity.
officer (AW-fih-sur) A person in charge of lower-ranking troops.
settlement (SEH-tul-ment) A place occupied by settlers.
volunteer (vah-lun-TEER) A person who works for free or agrees
    to perform a task.

WEB SITES

Due to the changing nature of Internet links, the Rosen Publishing Group, Inc., has developed an online list of Web sites related to the subject of this book. This site is updated regularly. Please use this link to access the list:

http://www.rosenlinks.com/fpah/jsut

PRIMARY SOURCE IMAGE LIST

Page 4: A map of Germany from the New York Public Library.
Page 5: A nineteenth-century view of Basel, Switzerland.
Page 6: George Clymer's Columbia Printing Press, circa 1817.
Page 8: An immigrant ship, from the *London Illustrated News*, 1850.
Page 9: *Swiss Infantrymen*, by Gianni Dagli Orti, 1840.
Page 11: Ships in New York Harbor.
Page 13: *Along the Santa Fe Trail*, an engraving in a book, now housed at the New York Public Library.
Page 15: A map of the western coast of America.
Page 17: A photograph of Sutter's Fort, New Helvetia, now with the Library of Congress.
Page 19: A lithograph by William E. Endicott, 1849, now with the Library of Congress.
Page 20: Portrait of Antonio Lopez de Santa Anna, 1858.
Page 21: American troops storming the Heights of Monterrey.
Page 23: Panning for gold in California.
Page 24: "An Account of California and the Wonderful Gold Regions," by J. B. Hall, 1849.
Page 25: Sutter's farm.
Page 27: John Augustus Sutter (1803–1880).

INDEX

ABOUT THE AUTHOR

Chris Hayhurst is a freelance writer living in Colorado.